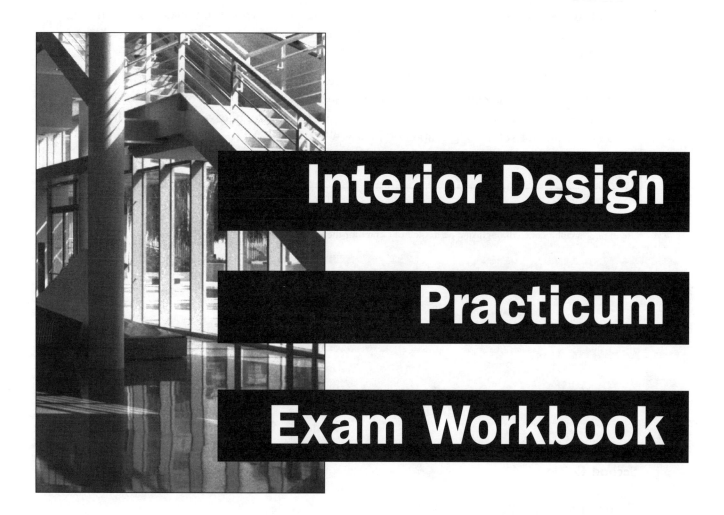

Interior Design

Practicum

Exam Workbook

Second Edition

Pamela E.B. Henley, ASID
NCIDQ Certified #9631

Professional Publications, Inc.
Belmont, CA

How to Locate Errata and Other Updates for This Book

At Professional Publications, we do our best to bring you error-free books. But when errors do occur, we want to make sure that you know about them so they cause as little confusion as possible.

A current list of known errata and other updates for this book is available on the PPI website at **www.ppi2pass.com**. From the website home page, click on "Errata." We update the errata page as often as necessary, so check in regularly. You will also find instructions for submitting suspected errata. We are grateful to every reader who takes the time to help us improve the quality of our books by pointing out an error.

Use of photograph granted through kind permission of Center for the Arts at Yerba Buena Gardens, San Francisco, CA, USA.

INTERIOR DESIGN PRACTICUM EXAM WORKBOOK
Second Edition

Current printing of this edition: 1

Printing History

edition number	printing number	update
1	1	New book.
1	2	Minor corrections.
2	1	Major revision. Copyright update.

Printed in the United States of America

Professional Publications, Inc.
1250 Fifth Avenue, Belmont, CA 94002
(650) 593-9119
www.ppi2pass.com

ISBN: 1-888577-82-7

Table of Contents

Preface

The *Interior Design Practicum Exam Workbook* is a direct offshoot of the thesis I prepared in pursuit of a Master of Arts degree in interior design at Marymount University in Fairfax, Virginia. The late Loren Swick, former president of the NCIDQ, mentored me on my thesis development. I'd hoped to carry the theme of my thesis further by publishing a study guide to aid other interior designers in their quest for NCIDQ certification. Having studied for and passed the NCIDQ exam myself, primarily through exam review courses, I knew there was a need for such a publication—an alternative or supplement to more expensive study courses that could offer candidates the flexibility to study singly or in a group setting.

Loren, who had been a contact for Professional Publications on other projects, referred the publisher to me in regard to a potential publication, which has now reached its second edition. This second edition is purely the result of recent exam revisions undertaken by the NCIDQ. This edition is a complete rework based on the new exam format; however, the overall structure of the publication remains the same.

I have endeavored to ensure that this guide is both relevant and applicable to the exam. Students from Marymount University and Mount Vernon College completed the sample exams of the first edition to verify the accuracy of the problems. For the second edition, various NCIDQ-certified professionals verified the integrity and efficacy of the workbook. I believe this workbook will be an effective study aid to help the reader achieve NCIDQ certification. Good luck!

It is my pleasure to thank those individuals who generously contributed their time and skills toward the completion of this publication. Thanks are due to several people at the National Council for Interior Design Qualification, to Karen Guenther for reviewing this manuscript, and to Loren Swick and Todd Bostick for their support in the development of the original manuscript. Christina Mastrantonio and Dennis Brownridge provided expertise in their review of metric conversions.

A special thank you to my editors, Elizabeth Fisher and Mary Fiala, for their guidance in the development of the first edition, as well as to all the staff at Professional Publications who were involved with this project. For the second edition of this book, my thanks go to Aline Magee, Cathy Schrott, and Heather Kinser of Professional Publications.

Lastly, I would like to thank Bob for proofreading, and Griffin and Devin for affording me the time to complete this manuscript.

Pamela E. B. Henley, ASID

Introduction

The design process is a performance consisting of the appropriate application of many skills. Professional designers are evaluated by how successfully they apply these skills to their clients' needs. The NCIDQ examination tests a candidate's minimum competency to apply the practical skills needed by interior designers.

This book will help you prepare adequately for the practicum portion of the exam. It includes a two-part design practicum sample problem along with its corresponding suggested solution, as well as additional information you will need to successfully complete the exam. Among the topics covered are barrier-free design, time management, the jury process, what to take to the test, the principles and elements of design, and drawing presentation techniques. Note that all names, locations, and situations in this book are fictional.

Completing the sample problem and reviewing the topics covered in this book will help increase your skills and knowledge, and thus decrease your apprehension about taking the exam. Even though this book cannot guarantee you a passing score, becoming familiar with the exam and its format will better enable you to perform with confidence.

THE NCIDQ

Formed in 1972 and formally incorporated in 1974, the National Council for Interior Design Qualification (NCIDQ) was created in the public interest to establish minimum competency standards for the interior design profession. The NCIDQ developed a certification examination designed to test for the knowledge and skills interior designers need in order to perform at acceptable professional levels.

The NCIDQ comprises members of regulatory agencies (from those states or provinces that have statutory requirements) and professional organizations including the American Society of Interior Designers (ASID), the International Interior Design Association (IIDA), and the Interior Designers of Canada (IDC). All of these organizations, with the exception of the Interior Design Educators Council, require passage of the NCIDQ exam for acceptance as a professional member.

THE IMPORTANCE OF PROFESSIONAL CERTIFICATION

Certification indicates to the public that interior design professionals have met an acceptable standard of professional education and experience, and that they can demonstrate a competent level of skill in key areas. Certification is used to protect the public from individuals who do not possess the knowledge to perform adequately, safely, and effectively. For this reason, achieving NCIDQ certification has become an important credential for design professionals.

Licensure also enlightens the public about the scope of the interior design profession and acknowledges the difference between an interior decorator and a Certified Interior Designer. Increasingly, states and Canadian provinces are licensing design professionals. All states and Canadian provinces that maintain certification laws require designers to pass the NCIDQ exam in order to use titles defined by their legislative acts, including Interior Designer, Registered Interior Designer, and Certified Interior Designer. In order to practice interior design in the District of Columbia, passage of the NCIDQ exam is required.

In addition, the certification exam serves as a self-policing function within the profession. Upon completion of a minimum of two years of work experience in combination with an educational program—a total of six years of educational and work experience combined—a designer becomes eligible for Interior Design Certification testing.

EXAM DEVELOPMENT

After reassessing the content of prior exams, NCIDQ based its 2000 exam revisions in part on the report titled *1998 Analysis of the Interior Design Profession*. While the knowledge being tested has not changed, the exam format has. Formerly in six parts, the exam has been restructured into a three-part format that emphasizes performance testing or practical experience rather than academic recall. NCIDQ has broken down the work of interior design into six performance areas and five critical issues. The performance areas are as follows.

Project Organization: comprises the organizational skills needed to guide a commercial project through all phases of the design process: knowledge of accessibility standards, financial management, marketing, client and public relations, and so on.

Programming: refers to gathering, interpreting, and integrating information identified through client and user needs analyses. These needs can include topics such as accessibility, codes, budget, spatial requirements, goals, existing elements, and project schedule.

Schematics: the process of transferring programmatic requirements into a graphic format. Results could include space plans, elevation and section drawings, and three-dimensional representations.

Design Development: involves all areas of design to be evaluated and refined toward a final design solution. After the development stage, the information can be transferred into its final form.

Contract Documents: the development of working drawings, schedules, and finishes. These documents are presented in a text and graphic format.

Contract Administration: includes issues pertaining to contract development; issues involving the owner, client, and contractor; contract administration; and interpretation of documents.

The five critical issues that NCIDQ focuses on, due to their impact on the work of interior design, are as follows.

Health and Safety: conforming to regulations, codes, and product performance standards, to protect the public safety.

Welfare: enhancing the social, psychological, and physical well-being of the community and the environment.

Function: interpreting programmatic information to meet design requirements.

Business, Law, and Ethics: applying industry and legal requirements to the interior design profession while employing ethical business practices.

Design Synthesis: interpreting project requirements and conditions to develop a design solution.

Table I.1. Overall Point Distribution for NCIDQ Exam

	Project Organization 11% total	Programming 14% total	Schematics 14% total	Design Development 20% total	Contract Documents 23% total	Contract Admin. 18% total
Health and Safety 18% total	1.6%	3.6%	3.2%	4.5%	3.6%	1.5%
Welfare 13.1% total	1.4%	2.5%	2.1%	3.0%	2.1%	2.0%
Function 29.5% total	1.6%	5.4%	4.0%	5.5%	8.0%	5.0%
Business, Law, & Ethics 26.9% total	5.7%	1.5%	1.7%	2.0%	8.0%	8.0%
Design Synthesis 12.5% total	0.7%	1.0%	3.0%	5.0%	1.3%	1.5%

EXAM FORMAT

Table I.1 gives the point distribution, by percentage, of each of the five NCIDQ critical issues, broken down by performance area. Refer to the NCIDQ website (www.ncidq.org) to verify these point distributions, since it is possible that they may change over time.

The NCIDQ exam is administered over a two-day period. It is rewritten prior to each new administration. The schedule shown in Table I.2 indicates the practicum portions of the exam in boldface.

Exams are administered twice a year, in April and October. Check the NCIDQ website for specific dates.

WHAT TO TAKE TO THE EXAM

- architect's scale
- 30/60- and 45-degree triangles
- templates (plumbing, circle)
- lead pencil with various leads
- highlighter
- eraser
- battery-powered calculator (without stored memory)
- pencil pointer or sharpener
- tracing paper, bumwad
- portable drafting table (24" × 36") if not available at the site
- beverages
- snacks
- tissue
- aspirin

Good luck on the exam!

Table I.2. NCIDQ Exam Schedule

time	activity
Friday	
8:00 a.m. – 8:30 a.m.	Instructions
8:30 a.m. – 12 noon	Section I: Principles and Practices of Interior Design (multiple choice, 150 questions, 3.5 hours)
12 noon – 1:30 p.m.	Lunch Break
1:30 p.m. – 2:00 p.m.	Instructions
2:00 p.m. – 5:00 p.m.	Section II: Contract Development and Administration (multiple choice, 125 questions, 3 hours)
Saturday	
8:00 a.m. – 8:30 a.m.	**Instructions**
8:30 a.m. – 12:30 p.m.	**Section III, Part 1: Schematics and Design Development (4 hours)**
12:30 p.m. – 2:00 p.m.	Lunch Break
2:00 p.m. – 2:30 p.m.	**Instructions**
2:30 p.m. – 5:30 p.m.	**Section III, Part 2 (3 hours)**

1 Design Practicum

The practicum portion of the exam, which was formerly in three sections, has been restructured into one section. It is, however, administered in two parts. Candidates are allotted four hours for the first part and three hours for the second part. The Practicum tests examinees' ability to analyze and interpret a written program and communicate that analysis through illustration. Candidates will receive an exam package for each section of the Practicum. This package includes all instructions and vellums necessary to complete the exam.

PRACTICUM, PART 1

For Part 1 of the Practicum, examinees are asked to develop a design solution for a multiuse space. This means the problem will involve both residential and commercial design.

Part 1 of the exam package includes the following.

- description of the project and corresponding code requirements
- site plan
- key plan
- exterior elevation
- adjacency matrix
- floor plan

- material and finish specifications
- material and finish schedule
- wall-type details
- solution package

Time Management

Because this exercise is complex, it is important to manage your time effectively by creating a study plan that is tailored to your needs and background. Be sure to time how long you take to complete each segment of this exercise. Keeping track of the time you spend on individual elements of the exercise will help you identify areas where you should increase your attention. For example, if you spent 45 minutes designing a rest room and 10 minutes designing a lunch room, you would need to practice designing rest rooms.

Make a copy of the Part 1 time-management worksheet provided and use it to record your progress through Part 1 of the sample exam. As you complete each segment, fill in how long it took. Then look carefully at how you spent your time. Once you have assessed your problem areas, continue to practice those elements until you have improved your competence and speed.

TIME-MANAGEMENT WORKSHEET FOR THE PRACTICUM, PART 1

item	allocated time	time spent
reading the program	15–20 minutes	_____
adjacency matrix	15–20 minutes	_____
bubble diagram	15–20 minutes	_____
rough floor and furniture plan	40–50 minutes	_____
final plans	50–70 minutes	_____
wall-type detail	5–10 minutes	_____
material and finish schedule	15–20 minutes	_____
review	10–15 minutes	_____
drawing enhancement	10–15 minutes	_____

After you complete the sample exam, assess the following.

1. Are barrier-free codes met?

2. Does the solution meet all the program requirements?

3. Is the presentation readable?

Before taking the real NCIDQ exam, try to allow enough time to practice and improve your skills. If you devote time to steady practice, the exam should seem more familiar when you actually take it. Also, refer to the Reading List at the end of this book for valuable references that will help you focus on the practicum problem.

Tips for the Practicum, Part 1

▪ Read the entire program description and program requirements twice before attempting a design solution. During the first readthrough, try to gain an overall understanding of what is required. During the second readthrough, highlight or make notes on important items. It will be hard to read the program twice because you will be concerned about the time constraints and feel an urgency to begin problem solving. But in the long run, you will probably find that the second reading enables you to avoid constantly referring back to the program.

▪ This program is concise and straightforward, and spatial relationships should quickly become clear to you. There are, therefore, only a few acceptable treatments of the space that can be developed within the time allotted to this exam section.

- Important items to note when reading the plans are
  - « the building itself and its orientation
  - « ceiling heights
  - « plumbing lines (be careful not to lay out your whole solution and then realize that the rest room is not accessible to a plumbing line)
  - « window, column, and load-bearing wall locations
  - « established ingress/egress routes
- Allow 15–20 minutes to read the program and review the key plan, site plan, and elevation.

Adjacency Matrix

The Practicum will require you to complete an adjacency matrix based on the project description. You will be given a blank matrix to be used for this purpose. It is important that you show primary and secondary adjacencies within the entire space. Not all rooms will be included on the matrix.

The sample matrix shown in Fig. 1.1 illustrates several spatial relationships. The dining room needs to be near the kitchen and somewhat close to the bathroom, but it does not need to be near the bedroom. The kitchen needs to be close to the den, but its adjacency to the bedroom is not important. The bedroom should be adjacent to the bathroom.

Design Process

Bubble Diagram

After reviewing the written program and building plans, you will begin to develop the design solution. The first step is completing a bubble diagram for your own use (this is not a requirement of the exam), keeping the following hints in mind.

Adjacency Matrix

● Direct/Primary Adjacency
○ Convenient/Secondary Adjacency

	1. Bedroom	2. Dining Room	3. Kitchen	4. Bath	5. Den
1. Bedroom					
2. Dining Room					
3. Kitchen		●			
4. Bath	●	○	●		
5. Den			○		

Figure 1.1 Sample Adjacency Matrix

- Be aware of views, plumbing access, ingress and egress routes, and architectural elements such as elevators, stairs, fireplaces, and so on. Start by placing the largest spaces that require window walls. Next, develop the diagram around areas that cannot be altered, such as plumbing chases and egress routes. Kitchen and bath areas should be placed within the specified distance of the plumbing lines. Reception and foyer spaces are usually somewhat centralized because they need to be placed near the main ingress/egress route. The main entrance should be located near a major public egress route or elevator.

- Place tracing paper over the floor plan of the building shell. Draw bubbles roughly to scale, leaving room for corridors and other circulation areas.

- Time yourself. The bubble diagram should take 15–20 minutes to develop.

Rough Floor and Furniture Plan

The next step is to begin the rough floor plan using your bubble diagram as a model.

- Keep your design solution simple. You will probably feel you should design creatively;

however, this exam does not test creativity. Rather, it tests your ability to make appropriate decisions on all aspects of design, to result in a simple and concise solution that is effectively communicated through graphics.

■ Avoid curvilinear or odd-angled walls and shapes. They are time consuming to draw, and it is difficult to develop a passable design solution with uncommon shapes.

■ Be sure to maintain a barrier-free environment in at least those areas of the program that require such an environment.

■ You can roughly sketch in furniture at this time.

■ You can draw the rough floor plan directly on the exam vellum sheet with a light lead weight and lightly applied pressure, or draw it on tracing paper, slid underneath the vellum and traced.

■ Time yourself. The rough floor plan should be completed in 40–50 minutes.

Final Plans

Now you are ready to move on to the final floor plan.

■ After establishing the floor plan, you can begin to think about furnishings in greater detail. In most cases, the candidate is not required to complete a furniture layout for every area. Always be sure to read the program and project description carefully. Address the required elements of the exam first, without getting caught up in drawing nonrequired elements. Use your time wisely.

■ Because minor changes may be made to the wall placement as you lay out your fixtures and furnishings, do not hardline (darken) your plan until it is laid out in its entirety. Read the program once more after you have designed your solution. If you are confident that you have met all the requirements, hardline or trace the final drawing on the exam vellum sheet. Refer to Ch. 4 for suggested techniques for drawing with various lead weights.

■ Label all rooms and storage areas, and any furnishings that might need explanation.

■ Draw all 5'-0" (1524 mm) accessible turning radii.

■ Label all square and lineal footage as specified by the project design requirements.

■ If you have time and want to dress up your drawing, you can poché (darken or fill in) walls, add texture (wood grain on tables, specks on carpet, and so on), or apply border treatments to carpet. Chapter 4 contains additional ideas, but this type of rendering is not required by the exam.

■ Time yourself. The final drawing should take 50–70 minutes to complete.

Wall-Type Details

Before your floor plan can be considered complete, you must specify wall types for one or more areas. The exam package illustrates several different wall-type details. You must select which wall type is most suitable for the specified area, and indicate that on the floor plan, following the directions in the exam program.

Material and Finish Schedule

The last step to address is completing the material and finish schedule. You will be provided with a material and finish schedule containing wall, floor, and ceiling materials. In addition, a blank schedule for some, but not all, of the rooms will be provided for you to fill in with the most appropriate finish/material. You must use only the specifications provided by the exam schedule.

Review and Drawing Enhancement

Before handing in Part 1 of the Practicum, take a moment to review the program and compare it against your design solution sheets to make sure you did not neglect anything. If you find areas that need attention, use your remaining time for drawing enhancements.

PRACTICUM, PART 2

For Part 2 of the Practicum, examinees are asked to complete a reflected ceiling plan, an electrical plan, and an elevation and section drawing.

The exam package for Part 2 of the Practicum includes the following.

- description of the additional scope of services and key plan
- key plan
- electrical legend
- floor plan
- equipment list
- elevation
- section
- reflected ceiling legend
- electrical plan
- reflected ceiling plan
- solution package

Time Management

Applying the same method as for Part 1 of the Practicum, you can use the Part 2 time-management worksheet to tailor your study plan to your needs.

Tips for the Practicum, Part 2

- Read the entire additional scope of services twice before beginning your design solution. During the second readthrough, highlight or make notes on important items. This program is much shorter than that of Part 1, so you should have no problem reading it even a third time if you so choose.

TIME-MANAGEMENT WORKSHEET FOR THE PRACTICUM, PART 2

item	allocated time	time spent
reading the program	15–20 minutes	_____
electrical plan	20–30 minutes	_____
elevation drawing	20–25 minutes	_____
section drawing	20–30 minutes	_____
reflected ceiling plan	20–30 minutes	_____
lighting fixture schedule	20–30 minutes	_____
review	10–15 minutes	_____

After you complete the sample exam, assess the following.

1. Does the solution meet all the program requirements?

2. Is the presentation readable?

- Allow 15–20 minutes to read the program and review legends, equipment lists, and drawings.

Design Process

Electrical Plan

The first step in developing the design solution is completing an electrical plan for those areas indicated on the electrical equipment list, keeping the following hints in mind.

- It is critical that you use the symbols illustrated in the electrical legend, which is included in your exam package.
- Note any specialty outlets and indicate all receptacle mounting heights.
- If you feel confident enough, start drawing directly on your vellum solution sheet.
- Time yourself. The electrical plan should take 20–30 minutes to complete.

Elevation and Section Drawings

The scope of services will require that an elevation and section drawing be provided for some type of custom furnishing. The floor plan will use an elevation symbol to indicate the elevation to be shown. The desired section view will be indicated by description.

- **Label, label, label!**
- Show all dimensions: width, depth, and height.
- Indicate all materials.
- Draw a section symbol on your elevation drawing.
- Time yourself. The elevation and section drawings should take 40–55 minutes total to complete.

Reflected Ceiling Plan and Lighting Fixture Schedule

You will be provided with a lighting description separate from the additional scope of services. This will give you specific information on the lighting wants and needs. You will be provided with a base plan that indicates furnishing locations, artwork, and so on. A legend will also be provided.

- Remember to locate lighting symbols in only those areas required by the program.
- Use only those symbols illustrated in the reflected ceiling plan legend.
- **Do not** alter any existing HVAC or sprinklers that are already shown on the plan.
- Draw switching diagrams for those areas specified.
- On the fixture schedule, use the concept notes area to explain how you have utilized various lighting types. For instance, use this area to justify a choice such as specifying a wall-wash fixture in order to accent a piece of artwork.
- Place emergency and exit lighting where required.
- If you feel confident enough, start drawing directly on your vellum solution sheet once you have developed a concept.
- Time yourself. You should be able to complete the reflected ceiling plan in 20–30 minutes, and the fixture schedule and concept notes in 20–30 minutes.

Review

Before handing in Part 2 of the Practicum, take a moment to review your drawings against the additional scope of services provided.

SCORING CRITERIA

Both parts of the practicum exam are scored by jury process. The jurors are professionals or educators who have already passed the NCIDQ exam. Individual jurors complete evaluation sheets that log whether each solution has or has not met the minimum requirements. The jury sheets are then compiled to indicate either a "pass" or "not passed" result. To ensure confidentiality, control numbers (instead of names) are used to track exams.

The judges use scoring criteria that are common to each practicum exam. A sampling of possible criteria, from the exam package, follows.

Adjacency Matrix

- Have primary adjacencies been met?
- Have secondary adjacencies been met?

Design Solution Sheet

- Are adjacencies correct?
- Are all required rooms shown?
- Are all required rooms labeled?
- Do all rooms meet correct size requirements?
- Are all doors graphically indicated?
- Are all door swings correctly indicated?
- Do egress doors open in the path of travel?
- Have all furniture, fixtures, and equipment (FF&E) been graphically indicated?
- Have all FF&E been scaled correctly?
- Are all required plumbing fixtures located properly?
- Are wall types indicated properly?
- Are all applicable code requirements met?
- Are all public and private spaces visually/acoustically separated per program requirements?
- Have all program requirements been met?
- Are the rooms functional?
- Is the overall plan functional?

Material and Finish Schedule

- In the 15 cells available, has the candidate selected the most appropriate finish/material for the floors, walls, and ceilings of a specific room? A total of five of these cells will be selected for scoring.

Elevation Drawing

- Does the elevation meet the project code requirements?
- Does the elevation meet floor plan and symbol orientation?
- Are the dimensions correct?
- Is the section symbol correct?

Section Drawing

- Are the height dimensions correctly indicated?
- Are the depth dimensions correctly indicated?
- Are materials adequate for the design solution?
- Does the section drawing match the elevation?
- Does the section drawing communicate the design intent clearly for construction?

Reflected Ceiling Plan

- Is the emergency lighting on the plan?
- Are fixtures used to implement various lighting functions correctly selected?
- Are fixtures used to implement various lighting functions correctly placed?
- Are fixtures used to implement various lighting functions correctly switched?

Electrical Plan

Five items from the electrical plan will be chosen for scoring based on two criteria.

- Is the correct symbol used for the indicated item?
- Is the symbol for each item placed correctly?

Keep these questions in mind as you develop your design, so you will be prepared to include all pertinent information in your final solution.

2 Design Practicum Sample Problem

SAMPLE PROBLEM, PART 1

Section III of the NCIDQ examination consists of Parts 1 and 2 of the Practicum. The first part of the Practicum is the most involved and is given a time limit of four hours. The second part is a smaller scale problem given a time allotment of three hours. As detailed in Ch. 1, you will be asked to design a solution for a multiuse space. All worksheets required for this problem are contained within this book.

INSTRUCTIONS

- Review the project description and code requirements.
- Review the following: key plan, site plan, and elevation.
- Review the project design requirements instructions and table.
- Complete the adjacency matrix.
- Complete the project design solution (floor plan) on the vellum provided.
- Review the material and finish specifications.
- Complete the material and finish schedule.
- Review the wall-type details.
- Indicate the wall types on the project design solution (floor plan).

Project Description

An established advertising firm named Great Expectations is relocating its headquarters to a new facility. You have been hired by the firm to create a space plan and furniture, fixture, and equipment (FF&E) layouts for the first floor of the space. The space is approximately 3500 ft² (325 m²) and is located in a downtown business district. The space comprises the following: reception area; large conference room; small conference/work room; file/copy area; lunch room; rest rooms; space for an office manager; library; storage room; space for three account executives and three support personnel; and a private bed and bath suite. The company also leases the second floor, which houses an office suite for the owner/principal of the company and substantial room for future growth of the company. Access to the second floor is either by the stairwell or the first floor elevator.

Staff have access to the building 24 hours a day, 7 days a week, by means of a security key card system. The company's reception area will require visitors' seating to accommodate 3–4 people, as well as a surface for literature. Approximately 10 linear feet (3048 mm) of wall space are required for display of the company's print advertisements. Visitors must be able to travel to the second floor via the stairs or elevator. There must be direct access to the conference rooms and rest rooms, and convenient access to the file/copy area and lunch room.

The office manager must have direct access to the support staff and file/copy area. The account executives require direct access to the support staff and library, and must be conveniently located near the office manager. The support staff are also direct users of the library and the file/copy room. A small conference/work room, which shall be utilized by the entire company, should provide direct access to the library.

A bed and bath suite is maintained for those personnel working odd hours. Sound insulation must be upgraded in this space.

Code Requirements

The following code requirements apply to this exam only and will be juried as such. These codes should be utilized in the development of your design solution.

- Two means of egress are required. When open in any position, doors shall not project more than 7" (178 mm) into the corridor.
- Egress (exit) doors must open in the direction of exit travel.
- Egress doors must be a minimum of 25'-0" (7620 mm) apart, measured along the interior path of travel.
- Paths of travel leading to an exit may not pass through a secondary space subject to closure by doors, storage materials, or other projections.
- All paths of travel must be barrier free and provide a 5'-0" (1524 mm) turning circle (illustrated as a dotted line) at changes of travel direction. Turning into a room does not require a turning circle. The minimum interior width of a corridor must be 44" (1118 mm). You must consider the open dimension of storage elements such as closet doors if you choose to locate them along the interior path of travel. The open dimension cannot hinder the required clear width path of travel.

- All door openings shall be at least 3'-0" (914 mm) wide with a 1'-6" (457 mm) clear space on the pull side of the door and a 1'-0" (305 mm) clear space on the push side of the door.
- All bathrooms must be barrier free with a 5'-0" (1524 mm) turning circle (illustrated as a dotted line). A door swing may encroach upon the turning circle a maximum of 12" (305 mm).
- Bathroom grab bars must be indicated, where required to provide accessibility, in appropriate locations on the plan. This includes two grab bars for a bathroom and three grab bars for an accessible shower.
- Sinks in rest rooms must have clear knee access.
- Flooring in rest rooms must be slip resistant.
- Walls in rest rooms must be impervious to moisture.
- All plumbing fixtures, including sinks, must be located within 20'-0" (6096 mm) of the plumbing access line. The plumbing access line is indicated on the floor plan.
- All sleeping rooms must have an operable window or an exterior means of egress.

Project Design Requirements

INSTRUCTIONS

- Include in your design solution all the items listed in the project design requirements chart.
- If an item does not include FF&E, you are not required to specify that area.
- Present your solution in either a drafted or free-hand sketch (to scale) format. The solution must be completed on the vellum worksheet provided.
- Draw and label all rooms, adhering to all adjacencies as described in the project description and the adjacency matrix.
- Draw all FF&E as noted in the project design requirements.

- Draw all walls, door swings, and other components that are part of the design solution, including all project code requirements.

- Draw all rest room plumbing fixtures and grab bars within the space. Draw and indicate dimensions for the 5'-0" (1524 mm) accessible turning radius.

- Indicate wall thickness.

- Label all square footage (square meters) and all lineal footage (lineal meters) as noted in the project design requirements.

- Ensure all spaces meet the minimum square footage (square meters) indicated in the project design requirements.

- Label for clarity.

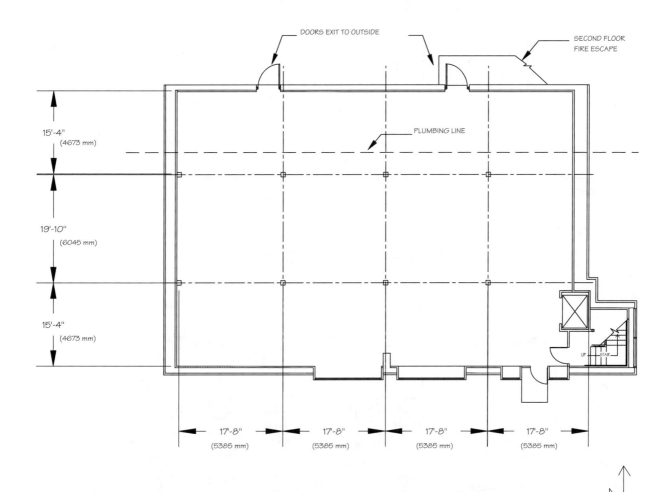

KEY PLAN

FIRST FLOOR
3500 SQ. FT. (325 m²)

SITE PLAN

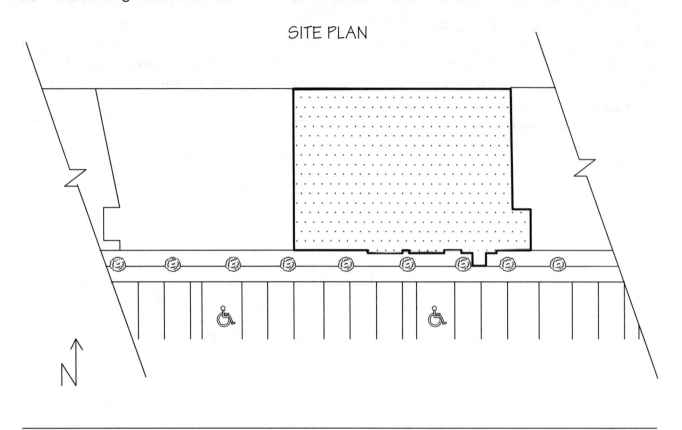

EXTERIOR NORTH ELEVATION

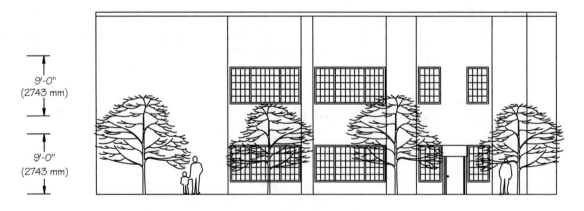

9'-0"
(2743 mm)

9'-0"
(2743 mm)

FLOOR TO SILL = 24" (610 mm)

FLOOR TO TOP OF WINDOW = 100" (2540 mm)

ALL WINDOWS ARE OPERABLE

PROJECT DESIGN REQUIREMENTS

ROOM NAME	MINIMUM AREA	FURNISHINGS	DIMENSIONS	NOTES
FIRST FLOOR				
Reception Area		three – four guest chairs		
		one end table		
		reception desk	min. 25 sf (2.3 m2) work surface	pencil drawer plus small lockable drawer
				min. 6 lineal ft (1828 mm) letter filing
				min. 6 sf (.56 m2) transaction counter
		display space		min. 10 lineal ft (3048 mm) wall space
Coat Closet	12 sf (1 m2)			
Conference Room	375 sf (35 m2)			
Men's Room	64 sf (6 m2)			
Ladies' Room	80 sf (7.4 m2)			
Lunch Room		two tables		min. 8 lineal ft (2438 mm) counter space
		eight chairs		min. 8 lineal ft (2438 mm) over counter cabinetry
		refrigerator	36 x 30 x 84 (914 x 762 x 2133 mm)	
		sink		
		dishwasher	24 x 24 x 24 (610 x 610 x 610 mm)	under counter placement
		microwave	21 x 18 x 18 (533 x 457 x 457 mm)	
File/Copy Room		file space		45 lineal ft (13716 mm)
		copier	36 x 24 x 30 (914 x 609 x 762 mm)	
		work counter		min. 30 sf (2.8 m2)
		shelving		15 lineal ft (4572 mm)
Storage Room	60 sf (5.6 m2)			
Support Staff	240 sf (22 m2)	open office area		
Account Executives	80 sf (7 m2) each	3 private offices		
Office Manager	150 sf (14 m2)	desk	36 x 72 (914 x 1828 mm)	
		credenza	24 x 72 (609 x 1828 mm)	
		shelf		6 lineal ft (1828 mm)
		two guest chairs		
		one task chair		
		files		15 lineal ft (4572 mm)
Library		table	36 x 72 (914 x 1828 mm)	
		6 chairs		
		bookcases		135 lineal ft (41158 mm)
Conf./Work Area	140 sf (13 m2)			
Bed/Bath Suite		sofa bed	75 x 26 (1905 x 660 mm)	
		cocktail table	24 x 36 (609 x 914 mm)	
		writing table	24 x 48 (609 x 1219 mm)	
		lamp		
Bathroom		toilet		
		sink		
		grab bars		
		accessible shower	72 x 36 (1828 x 914 mm)	
		counter area		min. 5 lineal ft (1524) counter-mtd. Sink

Adjacency Matrix

INSTRUCTIONS

- Do not fill in the shaded area.
- Using the project description, complete the adjacency matrix.
- Use the symbols presented to complete the matrix.
- Note that not all rooms are included in the adjacency matrix.

Material and Finish Specifications

INSTRUCTIONS

- Complete the material and finish schedule to represent the **most appropriate** finish/material.
- Use only the materials and symbols from the finish schedule.

Wall-Type Details

INSTRUCTIONS

- On the project design solution sheet, indicate the wall type for all walls in the bed and bath suite, including the bathroom.

Adjacency Matrix

● Direct/Primary Adjacency
○ Convenient/Secondary Adjacency

	1. Reception Area	2. File/Copy Room	3. Office Manager	4. Library	5. Conference Room	6. Rest Rooms	7. Support Personnel	8. Account Executives	9. Elevator
1. Reception Area									
2. File/Copy Room									
3. Office Manager									
4. Library									
5. Conference Room									
6. Rest Rooms									
7. Support Personnel									
8. Account Executives									
9. Elevator									

SYMBOLS	FLOORING MATERIALS
F1	Ceramic tile, glazed
F2	Brick
F3	Hardwood, wax finish
F4	Slate
F5	Ceramic tile, slip-resistant
F6	Carpet, 32 oz (946 cc) level loop glue-down
F7	Vinyl composition tile
F8	Carpet, 50 oz (1479 cc.) cut pile installed over pad
SYMBOLS	WALL MATERIALS
W1	Ceramic tile, glazed
W2	Latex paint, flat finish
W3	18 oz (532 cc) linen wallcovering
W4	Type II vinyl wallcovering
W5	Alkyd paint, enamel gloss
W6	Type I vinyl wallcovering
SYMBOLS	CEILING MATERIALS
C1	Gypsum wallboard (GWB)
C2	Acoustical tile, non-rated
C3	Mirror tile
C4	Wood tile

MATERIAL AND FINISH SCHEDULE

ROOM	FLOOR	WALLS	CEILING
LUNCHROOM			
CONFERENCE			
LADIES' ROOM			
RECEPTION			
MGR. OFFICE			

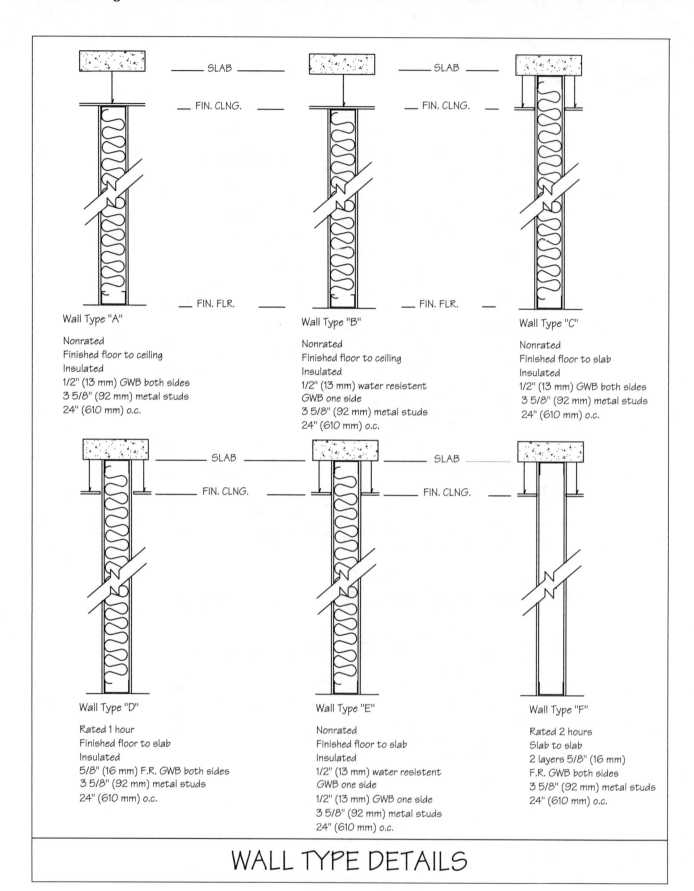

SLAB

FIN. CLNG.

FIN. FLR.

Wall Type "A"

Nonrated
Finished floor to ceiling
Insulated
1/2" (13 mm) GWB both sides
3 5/8" (92 mm) metal studs
24" (610 mm) o.c.

SLAB

FIN. CLNG.

FIN. FLR.

Wall Type "B"

Nonrated
Finished floor to ceiling
Insulated
1/2" (13 mm) water resistent
GWB one side
3 5/8" (92 mm) metal studs
24" (610 mm) o.c.

FIN. CLNG.

Wall Type "C"

Nonrated
Finished floor to slab
Insulated
1/2" (13 mm) GWB both sides
3 5/8" (92 mm) metal studs
24" (610 mm) o.c.

SLAB

FIN. CLNG.

Wall Type "D"

Rated 1 hour
Finished floor to slab
Insulated
5/8" (16 mm) F.R. GWB both sides
3 5/8" (92 mm) metal studs
24" (610 mm) o.c.

SLAB

FIN. CLNG.

Wall Type "E"

Nonrated
Finished floor to slab
Insulated
1/2" (13 mm) water resistent
GWB one side
1/2" (13 mm) GWB one side
3 5/8" (92 mm) metal studs
24" (610 mm) o.c.

Wall Type "F"

Rated 2 hours
Slab to slab
2 layers 5/8" (16 mm)
F.R. GWB both sides
3 5/8" (92 mm) metal studs
24" (610 mm) o.c.

WALL TYPE DETAILS

SAMPLE PROBLEM, PART 2

INSTRUCTIONS

- Review the additional scope of services.
- Review the key plan.
- Review the equipment list.
- Develop the electrical plan (voice, power, and data) on the vellum provided.
- Create the elevation and section drawings on the vellum provided.
- Review the lighting description.
- Develop the reflected ceiling plan on the vellum provided.
- Complete the fixture schedule on the vellum provided.

Additional Scope of Services

The principal and owner of Great Expectations has requested that you provide some additional services. The large office suite on the second floor requires elevation and section drawings, a reflected ceiling plan and fixture schedule, and an electrical plan. You have been asked to design an accessible reception desk and provide elevation and section drawings.

The reflected ceiling plan should provide various lighting concepts. Ambient lighting shall be provided throughout the space, with additional task and accent lighting.

An electrical, voice, and data plan indicating outlets needed for the equipment required (see the equipment list) must also be developed.

The power may be taken from the walls, floor, or ceiling.

Electrical Plan

INSTRUCTIONS

- Complete the electrical plan on the vellum provided.
- Make selections and mark accurate placement for telephone, voice, and data symbols required according to the equipment list.
- Indicate outlet heights and any specialty items.
- Use the symbols represented in the electrical legend. **Do not create your own symbols.**

Reflected Ceiling Plan

INSTRUCTIONS

- Complete the reflected ceiling plan and fixture schedule on the vellum provided.
- Do not remove or reconfigure existing equipment.
- Draw switching diagrams for all light fixtures on the vellum provided.
- Place emergency and exit lighting symbols on the vellum provided.
- In the fixture schedule on the vellum provided, under the heading "Concept Note," explain how you have utilized task, ambient, and accent lighting.
- Use the symbols from the reflected ceiling legend. **Do not create your own symbols.**

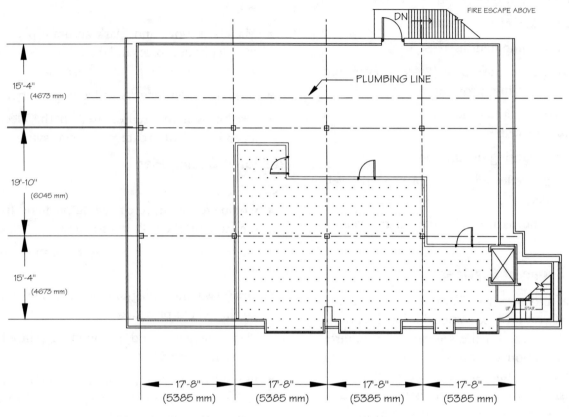

KEY PLAN

SECOND FLOOR

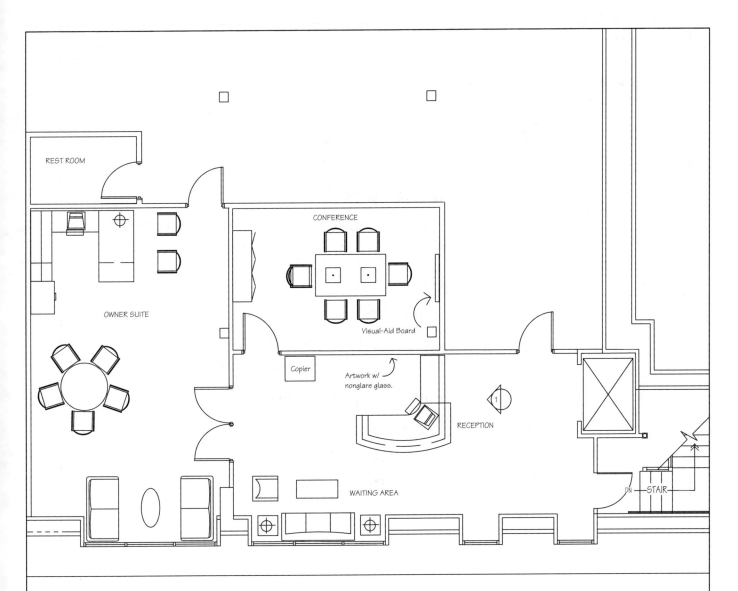

REST ROOM

OWNER SUITE

CONFERENCE

Visual-Aid Board

Copier

Artwork w/ nonglare glass.

RECEPTION

WAITING AREA

DN — STAIR

Equipment List:

Reception Area
- 1 computer with modem
- 1 laser printer
- 1 calculator
- 1 copier
- Under-counter task lighting
- 1 telephone
- Services to reception area equipment shall be mounted on the reception desk
- security card readers near egress routes

Waiting Area
- 2 table lamps

Conference Room
- 1 telephone

Principal/Owner Suite
- 1 computer with modem
- 1 laser printer
- 1 desk lamp
- 2 telephones

ELECTRICAL PLAN

SCALE: 1/8"=1'-0"

Electrical Symbols

⊖	Single Receptacle Outlet
⊖	Duplex Receptacle Outlet
⊕	Quadruplex Receptacle Outlet
⊕ GFI	Duplex Receptacle Outlet with GFI
◁	Telephone Outlet
◀	Data Outlet
◀	Data/Telephone Outlet
S	Security Card Reader
⊖	Floor Duplex Receptacle Outlet
◁	Floor Telephone Outlet
◀	Floor Data Outlet
△	Floor Special Purpose Outlet
P	Power Pole

Electrical Legend

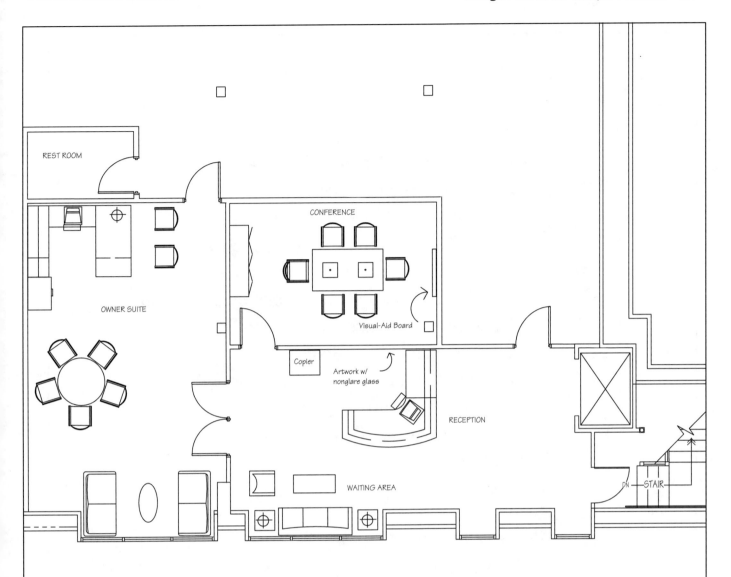

REST ROOM

OWNER SUITE

CONFERENCE

Visual-Aid Board

Copier

Artwork w/
nonglare glass

RECEPTION

WAITING AREA

DN ——STAIR

Lighting Description:

In the reception area, task lighting is required on the desk area. In addition ambient lighting should illuminate the space. Provide proper accent lighting for artwork.

Various lighting levels and fixtures are required in the conference room.

Exit and emergency lighting must be specified throughout the space.

Illustrate switching diagram for light fixtures.

REFLECTED CEILING PLAN   SCALE: 1/8"=1'-0"

Lighting Symbols

Walls	Ceiling	
⊢O	○	Surface-mounted Fixture, Incandescent
	®	Recessed Fixture, Incandescent
⊢O	○$_{LV}$	Surface-mounted, Low-voltage Incandescent
	®$_{LV}$	Recessed Fixture, Low-voltage Incandescent
	◖	Wall Wash Fixture, Incandescent or Compact Fluorescent
	⊕	Pendant Fixture, Incandescent or Compact Fluorescent
	─O─	Track Lighting, Incandescent
	▱	Surface-mounted Fluorescent
	▱$_R$	Recessed Fixture, Fluorescent 2x2 or 2x4
	⌞O⌟	Under-counter Fixture
	▱$_E$	Recessed Emergency Power
⊢O$_E$	○$_E$	Surface-mounted Fixture – Emergency
-Ⓙ	Ⓙ	Junction Box
⊢⊗	⊗	Exit Sign
	$	Single Pole Switch
	$$_3$	3-Way Switch
	$$_4$	4-Way Switch
	$$_D$	Dimmer Switch
	$$_{LV}$	Low-voltage Switch

Reflected Ceiling Legend

Professional Publications, Inc.

3 Barrier-Free Design and Space Configuraton

The information presented in this chapter applies to barrier-free design as it relates to the NCIDQ practicum section. The standards that will be discussed have been developed by federal agencies to conform with the American National Standard ICC/ANSI A117.1-1998, titled *Accessible and Usable Buildings and Facilities*. The NCIDQ exam tests your knowledge of codes that are used nationwide, not those pertaining to a particular county or state.

The 1992 passage of the Americans with Disabilities Act (ADA) has increased public awareness regarding accessibility issues. The ADA regulations, in most cases, correlate with ICC/ANSI A117.1-1998. The design issues regarding barrier-free interiors as tested in the NCIDQ Practicum concern the use of space by the visitor, employee, or resident. There are many other barrier-free and accessibility considerations not covered by the Practicum, such as hardware, alarm systems, and ergonomic considerations. However, these issues may be addressed in the multiple-choice section of the exam on barrier-free codes. For more specific information on these areas, refer to the *Interior Design Reference Manual* by David K. Ballast, AIA.

REQUIREMENTS FOR INTERIOR ACCESSIBLE ROUTES

According to the ADA and ICC/ANSI A117.1, an *accessible route* is a continuous unobstructed path connecting all accessible elements and spaces in a building or facility. The NCIDQ Practicum tests a candidate's knowledge of interior accessible routes, including corridors, floors, ramps, elevators, lifts, and clear floor space at fixtures. The NCIDQ Practicum does not address accessible routes of the exteriors of buildings, such as curb ramps, access aisles, lifts, ramps, and walkways.

A person with a physical disability is not necessarily confined to a wheelchair; however, most accessibility standards are based on the ability to operate a wheelchair within a given space. A nonambulatory disability is one that confines a person to a wheelchair, while a semiambulatory disability impairs walking. In addition, there are sight, hearing, coordination, and temporary (due to an accident) disabilities. The accessibility issues addressed most frequently by the Practicum are based on the operation of a wheelchair. The dimensions that will be discussed in this chapter are based on minimum requirements. Designers are not faulted for providing space beyond the minimum standards as long as all other space planning requirements have been met.

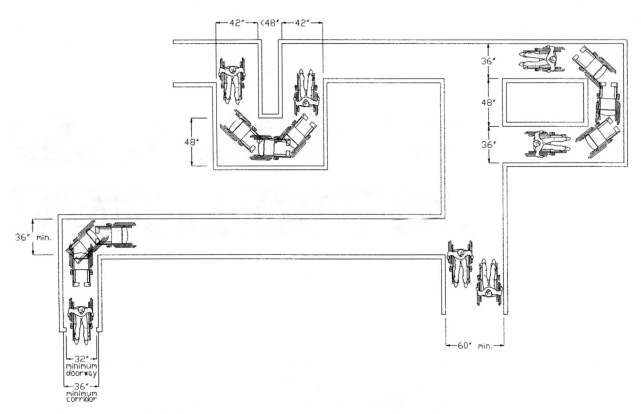

Figure 3.1 Barrier-Free Code Requirements

Figure 3.1 illustrates the following barrier-free codes, moving clockwise from the upper left-hand corner.

- *Width of accessible route for turns around an obstruction.* This configuration applies to a turn around an obstruction of less than 48" (1220 mm) wide. Dimensions of corridors are a minimum of 42" (1070 mm) with an increase to 48" (1220 mm) at the turnaround.

- *Width of accessible route for 90° turn.* This configuration demonstrates a 90° turn around a 48" (1220 mm) obstruction. Corridor dimensions are a minimum of 36" (915 mm) all the way around.

- *Minimum clear width for two wheelchairs.* The minimum width for two wheelchairs to pass one another is 60" (1520 mm).

- *90° turn—no obstruction.* A 90° turn without an obstruction requires a minimum of 36" (915 mm) for corridors.

- *Door clearance.* The minimum clear width for an accessible route is 36" (915 mm) continuously and 32" (810 mm) at a single point.

A 30" × 48" (760 × 1220 mm) clear floor space is required to accommodate a stationary wheelchair. Primary corridors 60" (1520 mm) wide must have a rest stop that meets the previously described dimensions after a maximum distance of 100 linear feet (2540 mm). It is doubtful that a practicum problem would have a corridor this long, considering the square footage of the problems given. As illustrated in Fig. 3.2, the standard requirement for a 360° turn is 60" (1520 mm) in diameter. An object such as a countertop may protrude 12" (305 mm) into the 60" (1520 mm) diameter clear space if the object is wall hung and meets ANSI height standards. See Fig. 3.3.

Door Clearances

The minimum clear width for a doorway is 32" (810 mm), with the depth of the doorway being a maximum of 24" (610 mm). See Fig. 3.4. If a circumstance requires a deeper area, the width of the doorway must be increased to 36" (915 mm).

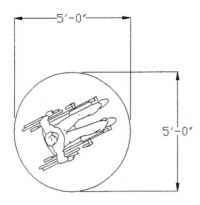

Figure 3.2 Requirement for 360° Turn

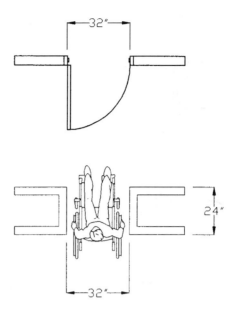

Figure 3.4 Minimum Clearance for a Doorway

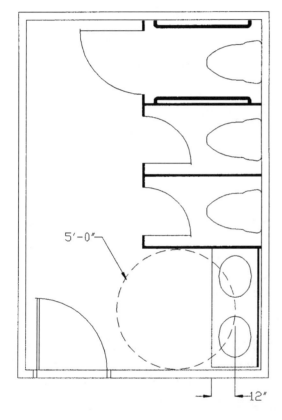

Figure 3.3 Requirement for Wall-Hung Objects

If a door threshold cannot be flush with the floor surface, it must be beveled on each side of the door and cannot surpass ½" (13 mm) in height. Figure 3.5 illustrates clearances for single doors and two-door vestibules.

Exits

The practicum section of the NCIDQ exam covers some information on exit criteria, but most of this information is tested by the multiple-choice portions of the exam. In most cases, the practicum program dictates which areas of the space require more than one exit. In order to ensure that safety requirements are met when placing more than one exit in a space, place exits at a minimum of one-half the maximum diagonal width dimension of the space in question. See Fig. 3.6.

The width of the exit door commonly used in the practicum section is 36" (915 mm). Areas such as theaters and restaurants require a larger exit because of their occupancy load. In most situations, the Practicum will require a maximum of two exits within the given required space.

In a residential dwelling, exit codes are not as strict as those in a commercial setting. A residential exit may pass through areas, including kitchens and laundry rooms, that are not considered acceptable for a commercial space.

Plumbing

Drinking Fountains

By law, at least one accessible drinking fountain is required in an accessible area on each floor of a building. Wall-hung and cantilevered units should have a clear knee space between the floor and bottom of the fountain of at least 27" (690 mm) high,

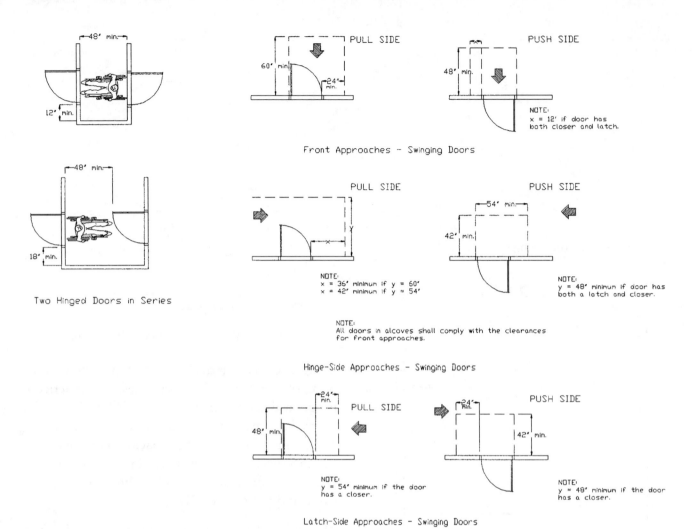

Figure 3.5 Clearances for Various Doorways

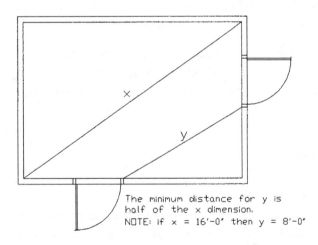

Figure 3.6 Requirements for Multiple Exits

30" (760 mm) wide, and 17" to 19" (430–480 mm) deep. A minimum clear floor space of 30" × 48" (760 × 1220 mm) is needed for a frontal approach by a wheelchair. See Fig. 3.7.

A unit without clear space below must have a clear floor space of 30" × 48" (760 × 1220 mm) to allow a person to make a side approach. See Fig. 3.7.

Toilet Stalls

As indicated in Fig. 3.2, a 60" (1520 mm) diameter clear floor space is required for the maneuverability of a wheelchair. In addition, accessible toilet stalls should stem from an accessible route.

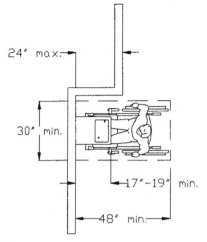

Wall-Mounted Fountain

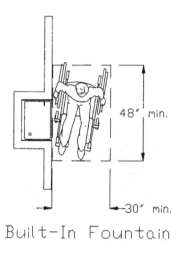

Built-In Fountain

Figure 3.7 Drinking Fountain Requirements

As shown in Fig. 3.8, there are many acceptable configurations of toilet stalls. The design varies depending on whether the water closet is floor mounted or wall hung. The floor-mounted water closet requires four additional inches of clearance space. In a situation where a toilet stall is not used, the toilet must be placed 18" (460 mm) on center from an adjacent wall.

Toilet Room Doors

Doors must provide a minimum clear opening of 32" (810 mm) and must swing out from the toilet stall. In a toilet room that provides a space 36" (915 mm) wide by the depth of the stall, in addition to the 60" (1520 mm) diameter turning space, a door may swing into the room. See Fig. 3.9.

Toilet Room Hardware

Grab bars are mounted 33" to 36" (840–915 mm) above the finished floor and, in most cases, are mounted on the back and side of the water closet. Some situations require grab bars to be mounted on both sides of the water closet. See Fig. 3.8.

Urinals

A clear floor space of 30" × 48" (760 × 1220 mm) must be provided in front of a urinal to allow for a forward approach. This space can overlap or adjoin an accessible route. The urinal must be either wall hung or a stall type with an elongated rim, mounted a maximum of 17" (430 mm) above the finished floor.

Shower Stalls

Two types of accessible shower stalls are illustrated in Fig. 3.10. The first type requires a bench to be mounted 17" to 19" (430–480 mm) above the finished floor and to run the entire depth of the stall. Grab bars are mounted on the faucet control wall and the adjacent wall. The second shower type (the size of a standard bathtub) does not have a bench, so that a wheelchair can enter the shower. Grab bars surround all three shower walls.

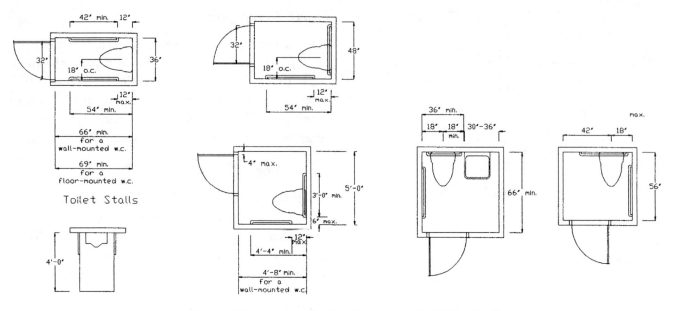

Figure 3.8 Acceptable Configurations for Toilet Stalls

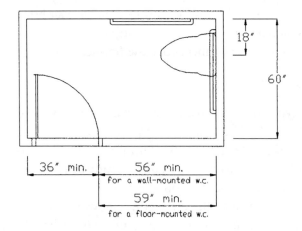

Figure 3.9 Standard Stall at End of Row or
Toilet Room with In-Swinging Door

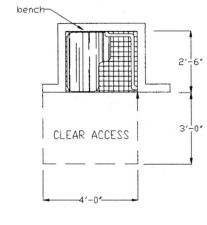

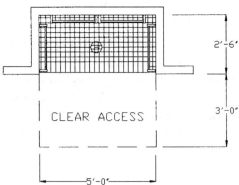

Figure 3.10 Shower Stall Requirements

TYPICAL SQUARE FOOTAGES AND SPACE CONFIGURATIONS

Table 3.1 and Figs. 3.11–3.18 reflect areas that recur most frequently in the Practicum. The square footages shown here can be used as estimates in your planning. However, be aware that the practicum program requirements may specify the exact amount of space required for an area. The requirement of the practicum program would then supersede the estimates given in Figs. 3.11–3.18.

It would be impossible to remember square-footage approximations for every space, but the sample test and day-to-day work experience should make you more familiar with estimating spatial allowances.

Table 3.1 Area Square-Footage Requirements

area	square footage/(meters)	area	square footage/(meters)
bathrooms		*public spaces (cont.)*	
water closet with lavatory	20–30 ft² (1.9–2.8 m²)	general office staff	68–100 ft² (6.3–9.3 m²)
water closet, lavatory, and tub (residential, nonaccessible)	35–45 ft² (3.3–4.9 m²)	manager	100–150 ft² (9.3–14 m²)
residential		conference room	20–30 ft²/person (1.9–2.8 m²/person)
kitchen	65–125 ft² (6.0–11.7 m²)	*conference table seating*	
living room	150–400 ft² (14–37 m²)	assembly room	10–15 ft²/person (0.9–1.4 m²/person)
dining room	75–250 ft² (6.9–23.2 m²)	auditorium	6–10 ft²/person (0.5–0.9 m²/person)
master bedroom	120–200 ft² (11.1–18.6 m²)	lounge (lobby)	20–30 ft²/person (1.9–2.8 m²/person)
bedroom	90–100 ft² (8.4–9.3 m²)	hospital room	75–90 ft² (6.9–8.4 m²)
public spaces		executive offices	200–300 ft² (18.6–27.9 m²)
reception area	15–25 ft²/person (1.4–2.34 m²/person)	hotel room	100–175 ft² (9.3–16.3 m²)
secretarial	54–88 ft² (5.04–8.2 m²)		

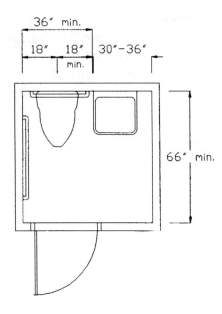

Figure 3.11 Half Bath

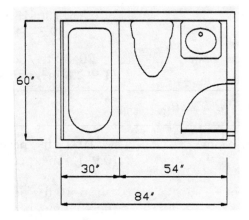

Figure 3.12 Full Bath

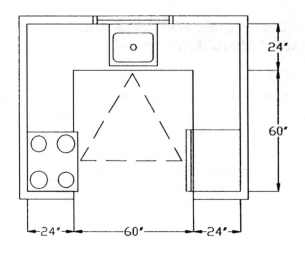

Figure 3.13 Kitchen

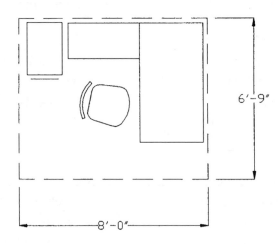

Figure 3.14 Secretarial Workstation

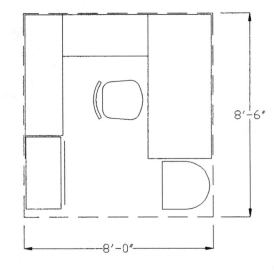

Figure 3.15 General Office Staff Work Space

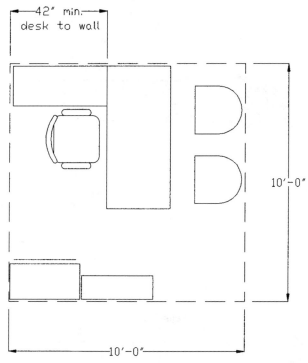

Figure 3.16 Management-Level Work Space

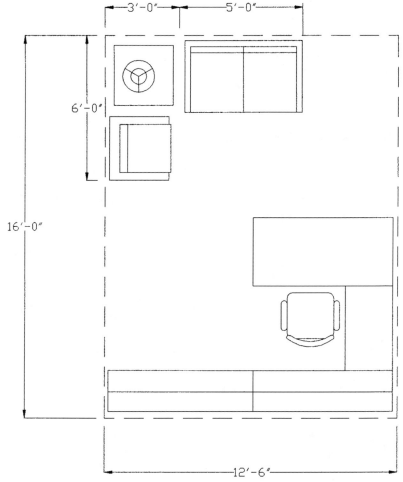

NOTE:
A 42" round table and 4 chairs
can be used as an alternative
to lounge seating.

Figure 3.17 Executive Office Work Space

Round Tops

Diameter inches	Approximate seating
42	4
48	5
54	6
60	7
66	7
72	8
84	9
96	11

Square Tops

Dimensions inches	Approximate seating
36×36	4
42×42	4

Rectangular Tops

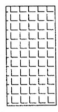

Dimensions inches L W	Approximate seating
48×24	4
60×24	4
72×24	6
84×24	6
96×24	6
60×30	4
72×30	6
84×30	6
96×30	8

Racetrack Tops

Dimensions feet L W	Approximate seating
10×10	12
12×5	12
15×5	16

Figure 3.18 Conference Table Seating

Professional Publications, Inc.

4 Design Presentation

This chapter presents drawing techniques that will help you both during and long after you have passed the NCIDQ exam. The NCIDQ exam does not specifically test drawing skills. The practicum section, however, requires a graphic presentation that must be legible and understandable to the jurors. Although you must meet all the required objectives to pass the exam, regardless of how your final solution is presented, a drawing that is highly readable and visually interesting will be received positively by the jurors. Consider spending time prior to taking the exam practicing drawing skills at work and on sample tests to achieve the best presentation results possible while still meeting all the exam objectives.

LINE QUALITY

It is a good idea to use a variety of line weights in the final practicum solution. This makes your drawings more interesting while increasing their readability. Because you will use vellum sheets to present the drawing solution, a pencil lead is the advisable presentation medium. Experiment with different lead weights before the exam to determine what works best with your personal drawing style and hand pressure. Use the following weights as a guideline.

- *Walls:* Draw with the darkest leads: F, H, or HB. To avoid smudging, do nor darken walls until the drawing is ready to be finalized for presentation.
- *Furniture, fixtures, and equipment:* Draw these elements in a medium 2H or 3H lead.
- *Drawing accents:* These include area rugs, plants, wood grain, and so on. Use a light-weight lead, such as 4H or 5H, for these items.
- *Shadows:* Use a dark lead, but a lighter weight than that used for the walls. For instance, if the walls are drawn in HB, use an H lead for shadows.
- *Poché:* The term *poché* signifies the filling in of walls. To avoid smudging, fill in walls on the reverse side of the drawing. Use a dark lead.

TEMPLATES

Templates may be used for the NCIDQ exam; however, there are some drawbacks to using templates in drawing solutions because they often cause inconsistencies in line weights. Also, the use of a template does not allow you to express your personal drawing style. Templates are most useful for drawing door swings (a circle template) and for providing a basis for furniture drawings. A sofa can be quickly mapped out with a rectangle template and expanded upon in the final drawing stage. Remember, free-hand drawing is an acceptable form of drawing presentation on the exam.

PRESENTATION TECHNIQUES

Figures 4.1–4.3 show different ways of presenting one aspect of a drawing. Figure 4.1 illustrates a table and chair combination. From left to right, the first example is an acceptable representation, but it lacks interest. The middle example is visually more interesting because of the patterned tabletop and the chair placement. The final example, a glass-top table, is the most visually stimulating. The drawing illustrates different line weights, with the chair portions underneath the table drawn lighter and with the illusion of glass, a plant, and different chair positions. It should be stressed that the first example is acceptable and further enhancements should not be attempted until the entire drawing is complete.

Figure 4.2 illustrates the transformation of a rectangular box loveseat into a sofa that has curves, depth, and pattern. The first example, on the far left, is

adequate for passing the exam. The difference in the visual effect of the beginning and end results is apparent in this example. The sofa begins as a rectangle, but through the addition of curves, lines (wrinkles), pattern, and shading, it emerges as a piece of furniture that looks like someone might actually sit on. In addition, readability of the drawing has markedly increased.

FINISHES

Finishes represented so far have consisted of glass, patterned fabric, and laminate (table). The finishes that can be represented in the NCIDQ exam are limited only by the time available and your talents as an illustrator. Figure 4.3 presents some of the more common finishes represented in the exam. Other examples will be illustrated later in this chapter.

PRESENTATION OF A ROOM

Figures 4.4–4.6 demonstrate the transformation of a room from its most simple form (acceptable by NCIDQ) to one that is much more eye-catching. Figure 4.4 presents an office with basic

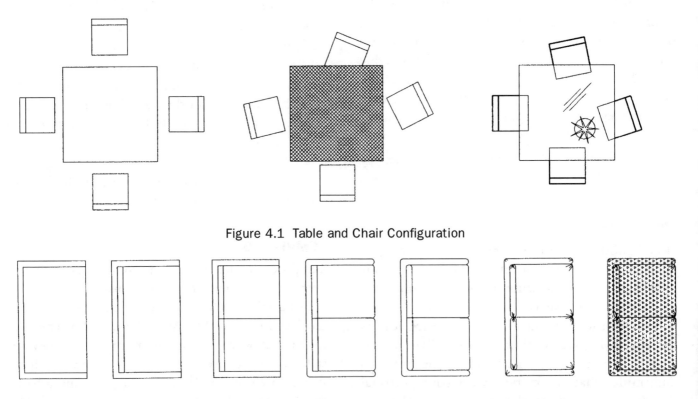

Figure 4.1 Table and Chair Configuration

Figure 4.2 Transformation of a Loveseat

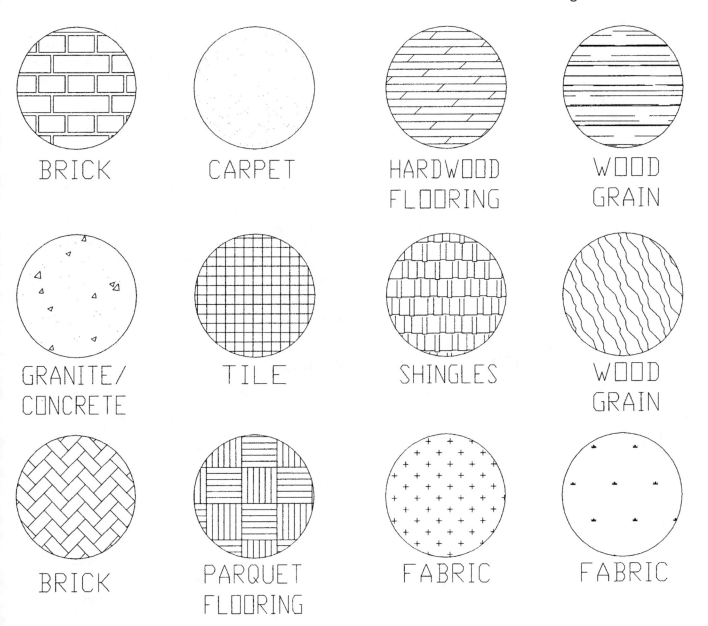

Figure 4.3 Sample Finishes

template-like furnishings. The representation is acceptable, but if time allows, you can create a more exciting visual impression. Figure 4.5 enhances the drawing with the use of wood grain on the desk and bookcase, a phone, an indication of the number of file drawers, and the introduction of shadow. Figure 4.6 shows a company space that expands on the previous single office. The additions made to Fig. 4.6 are the area rug and hardwood flooring. In addition to the visual variety these items bring to the overall illustration, they also represent two different textures—that of the hardwood flooring, and that of the fringe on the rug. The area rug also introduces more pattern.

Figure 4.7 depicts an office in the simplest form that would be passable for the exam.

The addition of plants, a textured conference table, and some shading further enhance the appearance of the office. See Fig. 4.8.

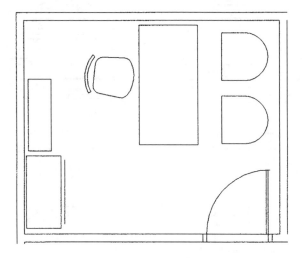

Figure 4.4 A Basic Office

Figure 4.5 Improved Drawing

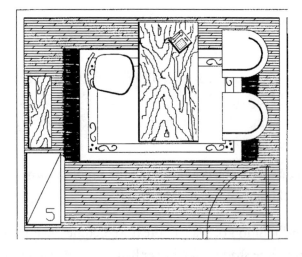

Figure 4.6 Enhanced Drawing of Office

Figure 4.9 illustrates ways to add flooring materials. Borders and tile are two quick additions that can strengthen the appearance of the space and add texture.

Wood grain, additional shadows, and plants increase the visual effectiveness of the space. See Fig. 4.10.

The next version of the office displays shadows on all furnishings, the addition of hardwood flooring, and an area rug. See Fig. 4.11. Speckles (dots made with pencil lead) represent carpeting throughout the space. Figure 4.12 displays walls in a pochéd format. This technique is very effective in highlighting each room. Pochéd walls make a solution easier for the jurors to read.

SHADOWING

Use the following techniques to achieve the shadowing style that was introduced in the previous examples. Either the west and south, the north and east, the north and west, or the east and south sides of an object should be hardlined in a darker lead: H or HB. Figure 4.13 illustrates the shadowing technique seen in the previous drawings, while Fig. 4.14 introduces a new method.

Shadowing should be one of the last additions to a drawing. It is a good idea to practice a shadowing technique before going into the exam. The shadows must conform to one style and follow the same direction to make this drawing enhancement technique effective.

THE FINAL DRAWING

The walls and shadows should be the last items completed on the final drawing. Since these two items use darker leads, saving them for last will reduce smudging. Work from the top of the drawing downward so your hands will not contribute to smudging. If you choose to poché walls, do it on the reverse side of the drawing.

Even though the majority of exam candidates will not be able to complete a test drawing to the degree

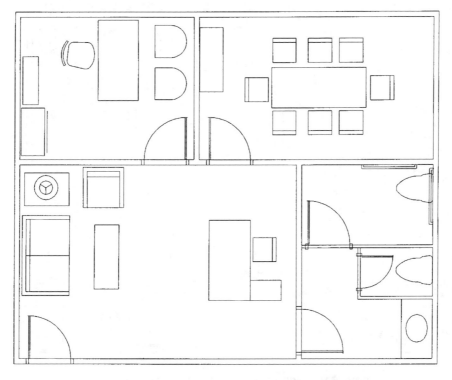

Figure 4.7 Simplest Acceptable Office for Exam

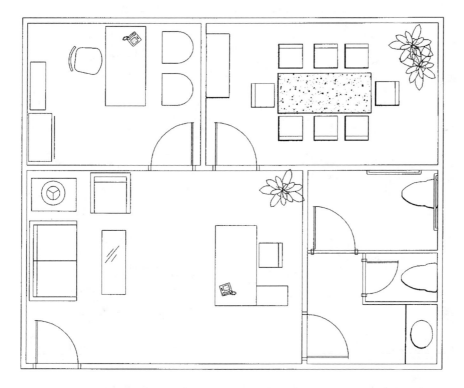

Figure 4.8 Enhanced Office

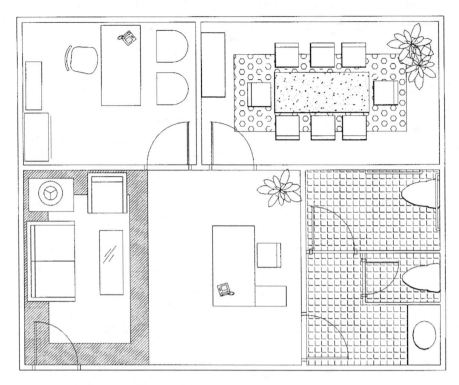

Figure 4.9 Additional Flooring Materials for Office

Figure 4.10 Additional Finishes Represented in Office

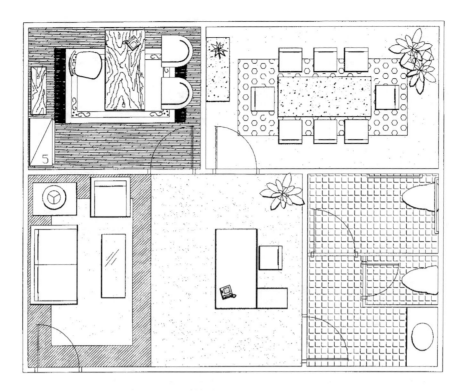

Figure 4.11 Office with Enhanced Textures and Shading

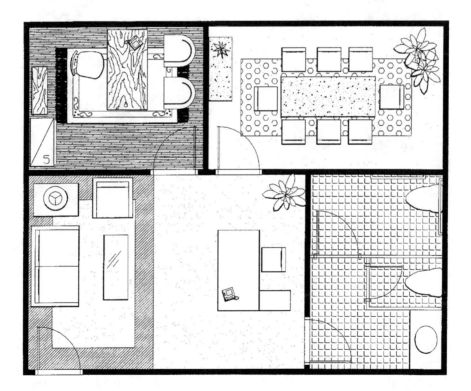

Figure 4.12 Office with Pochéd Walls

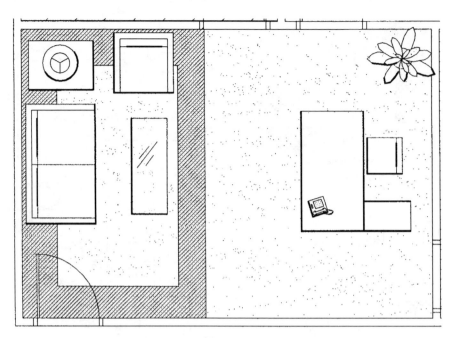

Figure 4.13 Shadowing Technique

Figure 4.14 Alternate Shadowing Technique

shown in Fig. 4.10, these presentation techniques may be used to increase the quality of drawings in your everyday work environment and are worthwhile skills to acquire.

Remember, *none of these techniques is needed to pass the NCIDQ Practicum*. These techniques serve only to increase the readability and visual excitement of your graphic solution.

Design Practicum

Solution

SOLUTION FOR PART 1

Adjacency Matrix

Figure 5.1 illustrates the spatial adjacencies dictated by the written program. Candidates were asked to leave the grayed areas blank. Not all rooms were represented on the matrix; therefore, not every adjacency was required.

Adjacency Matrix ● Direct/Primary Adjacency ○ Convenient/Secondary Adjacency	1. Reception Area	2. File/Copy Room	3. Office Manager	4. Library	5. Conference Room	6. Restrooms	7. Support Personnel	8. Account Executives	9. Elevator
1. Reception Area									
2. File/Copy Room	○								
3. Office Manager		●							
4. Library									
5. Conference Room	●								
6. Restrooms	●				○				
7. Support Personnel		●	●	●					
8. Account Executives			○	●			●		
9. Elevator	●				●	●			

Figure 5.1 Completed Adjacency Matrix

Graphic Design Solution

The following pages trace the development of the graphic design solution from the initial bubble diagram to the final solution. The solution is presented in a combination sketched and drafted format. Solutions to this problem will vary from person to person. Solutions that pass are those that meet the requirements of the program correctly. Obviously, in a real work situation a designer would allot more than four hours to a project of this size. Remember that for purposes of the exam, it is important to create a passing solution even if it is not the best or most complete real-world solution.

Figures 5.2–5.6 illustrate the progression of the design process for this design portion of the Practicum. Figure 5.7 illustrates a block plan for an alternate design solution.

DESIGN PROCESS PROGRESSION

1. Begin by diagramming spatial relationships. Remember to place those areas requiring plumbing a maximum distance of 20'-0" (6096 mm) from the plumbing line to the intended source. See Fig. 5.2.

2. Determine ingress/egress routes. Sketch walls, placing larger spaces first. See Fig. 5.3.

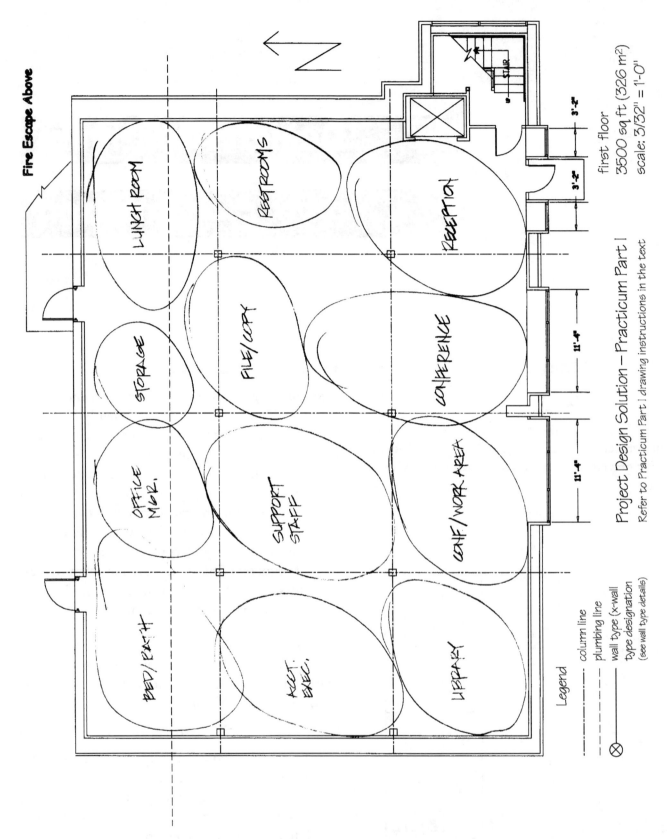

Figure 5.2 Project Design Solution (Bubble Diagram)

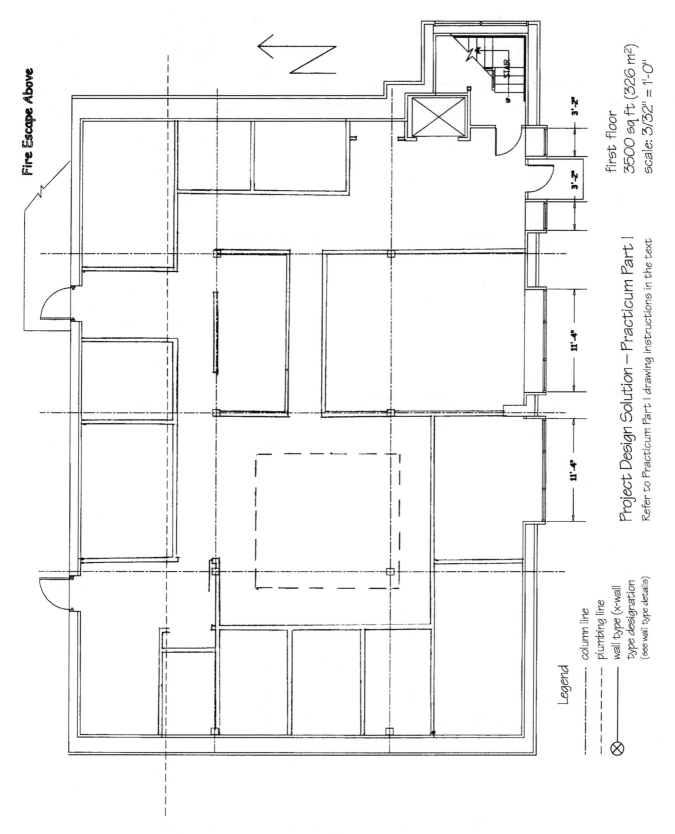

Figure 5.3 Project Design Solution (Rough Floor Plan—Early Stages)

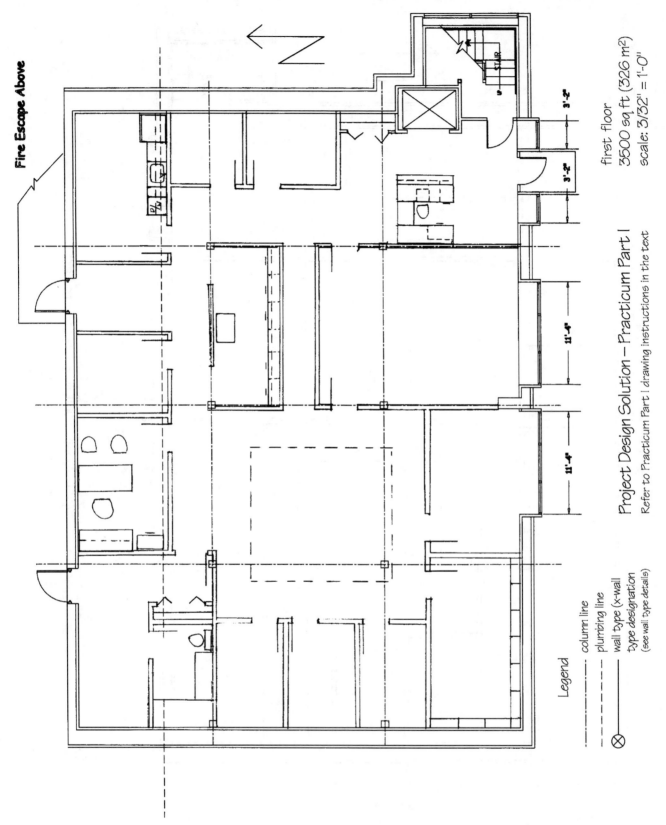

Figure 5.4 Project Design Solution (Rough Floor Plan—Late Stages)

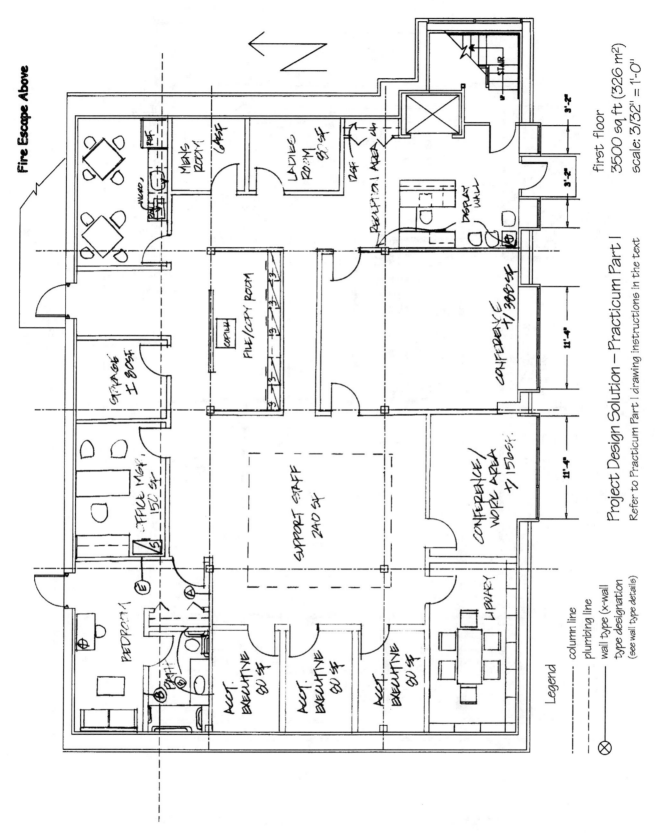

Figure 5.5 Project Design Solution (Final Floor Plan—Early Stages)

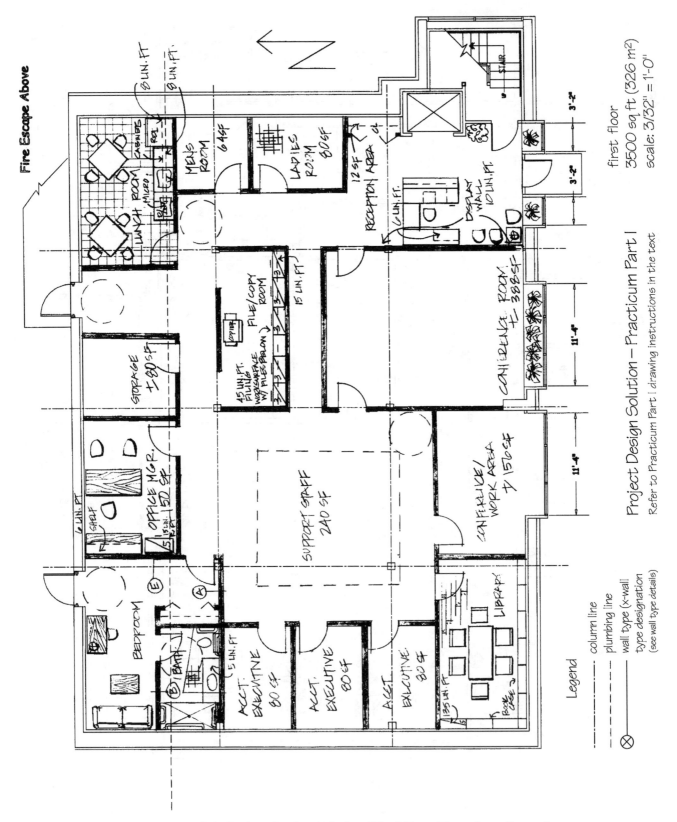

Figure 5.6 Project Design Solution (Final Floor Plan—Late Stages)

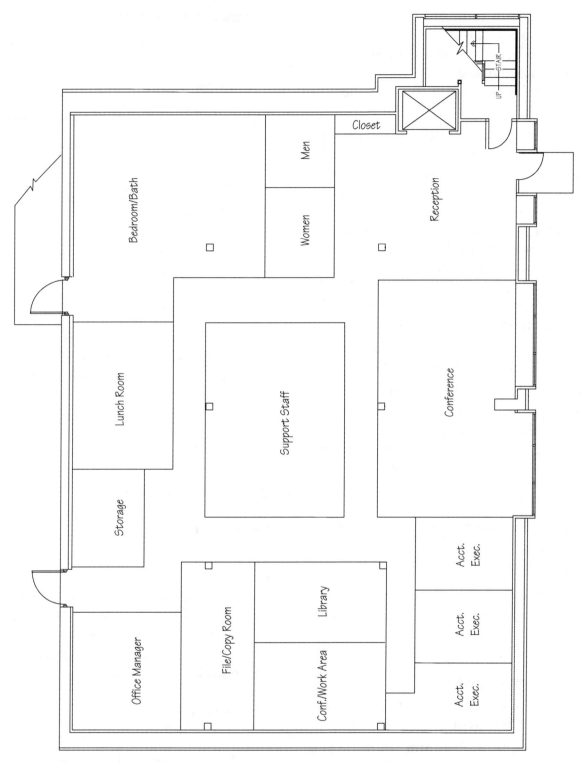

Figure 5.7 Block Plan for an Alternate Design Solution

3. Place only those furnishings required by the program. Make sure all code requirements are being met. The bath should be sketched, as well as kitchen counter area and furnishings for the office manger and receptionist. See Fig. 5.4.

4. Make sure all code requirements are met. Alter the kitchen doorway to allow 1'-6" clear space on the pull side of the door. Add tables in the kitchen. Place only those furnishings that are required by the program. Allow the required space for account executives and support staff. Place furniture in the library, copy/file room, and bedroom. Begin to place notes and label all rooms. Add grab bars in the bathroom. Label all square footage/square meters as required by the project description. See Fig. 5.5.

5. Add wall types to the bed/bath suite as required by the design program. See Fig. 5.5.

6. Add all remaining pieces of furniture required by the project description. Add notes, including numbers on files to indicate number of drawers, display walls in the reception area, shelving, and so on. See Fig. 5.6.

NOTES ON SOLUTION

- The required ingress/egress routes are present.
- All areas of the plan are labeled (e.g., RECEPTION AREA).
- The plan meets barrier-free codes.
- Furnishings are labeled where required for clarity.
- Furniture is placed only in those areas dictated by the project description.
- The kitchen and bathrooms are placed within 20'-0" (6096 mm) of the plumbing line.
- Enhancements—such as bath tile, wood grain on desks, plants, and the detail of the copy machine—are made to the drawing.
- All areas with required square or lineal footage have been labeled.
- Walls have been shaded to increase readability of the drawing.

Material and Finish Schedule

The material and finish schedule shown in Fig. 5.8 indicates the most appropriate choices for each particular space.

MATERIAL AND FINISH SCHEDULE

ROOM	FLOOR	WALLS	CEILING
LUNCHROOM	F7	W6	C2
CONFERENCE	F8	W3	C1
LADIES' ROOM	F5	W1	C2
RECEPTION	F6	W2	C1 or C2
MGR. OFFICE	F6	W2	C2

Figure 5.8 Completed Material and Finish Schedule

Wall-Type Details

After wall types have been added to the bed/bath suite as required by the design program, wall-type details are placed on the floor plan of the graphic design solution. The bathroom wall must be impervious to moisture per the project code requirements. The design program requires that sound insulation be upgraded in the bed/bath suite.

SOLUTION FOR PART 2

Electrical Plan

All the following comments refer to Fig. 5.9.

- The symbols shown on the electrical legend provided have been used. The electrical plan solution illustrates all power, voice/data, and telephone outlets in correspondence with the provided equipment list.
- Security card readers have been specified in egress areas.
- All outlet heights have been labeled. Outlets that are included in built-in furniture are located at desk height.
- Quadraplex receptacles have been used on the reception desk to accommodate multiple electronic devices.

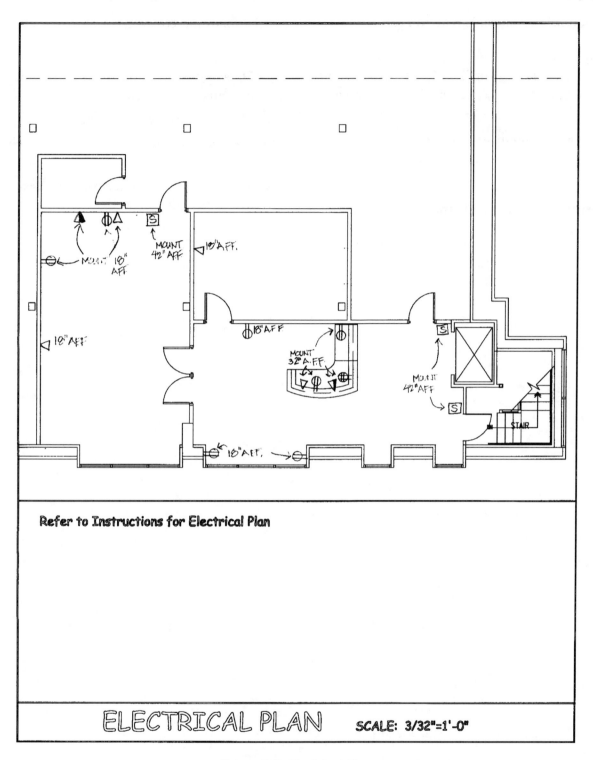

Refer to Instructions for Electrical Plan

ELECTRICAL PLAN   SCALE: 3/32"=1'-0"

Figure 5.9 Electrical Plan

Reflected Ceiling Plan

All the following comments refer to Fig. 5.10.

- The fixture schedule is complete and briefly describes the use of TASK, AMBIENT, and ACCENT fixtures as required per the instructions.
- Exit sign symbols are located at egress routes.
- Switching diagrams are present.
- Fixture legend symbols are used.
- Existing HVAC and sprinklers were **not** moved.

Elevation and Section Drawings

All the following comments refer to Figs. 5.11 and 5.12.

- Dimensions for width, height, and depth are indicated as required.
- Materials have been labeled.
- The section symbol is shown on the elevation drawing.
- The section is illustrated for the accessible area of the reception desk.

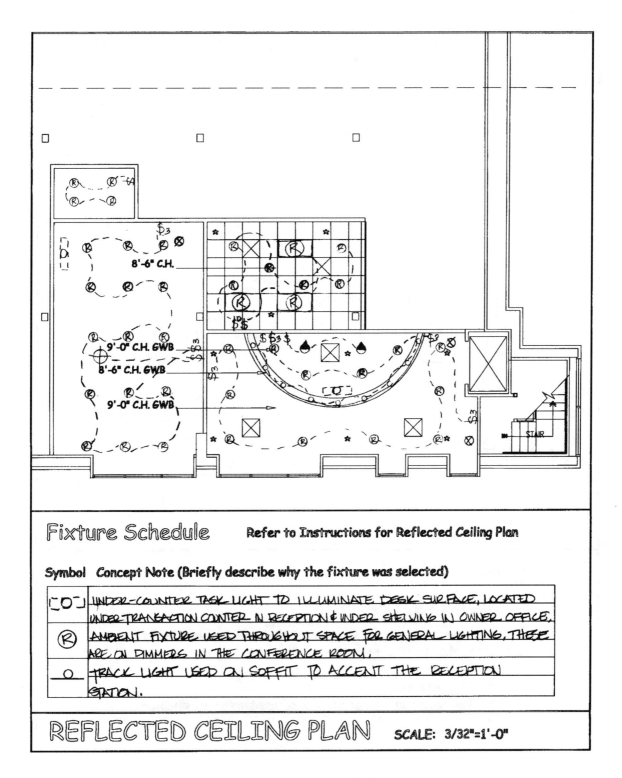

Fixture Schedule   Refer to Instructions for Reflected Ceiling Plan

Symbol   Concept Note (Briefly describe why the fixture was selected)

Symbol	Concept Note
[O]	UNDER-COUNTER TASK LIGHT TO ILLUMINATE DESK SURFACE, LOCATED UNDER TRANSACTION COUNTER IN RECEPTION & UNDER SHELVING IN OWNER OFFICE.
Ⓡ	AMBIENT FIXTURE USED THROUGHOUT SPACE FOR GENERAL LIGHTING, THESE ARE ON DIMMERS IN THE CONFERENCE ROOM.
O	TRACK LIGHT USED ON SOFFIT TO ACCENT THE RECEPTION STATION.

REFLECTED CEILING PLAN   SCALE: 3/32"=1'-0"

Figure 5.10 Reflected Ceiling Plan

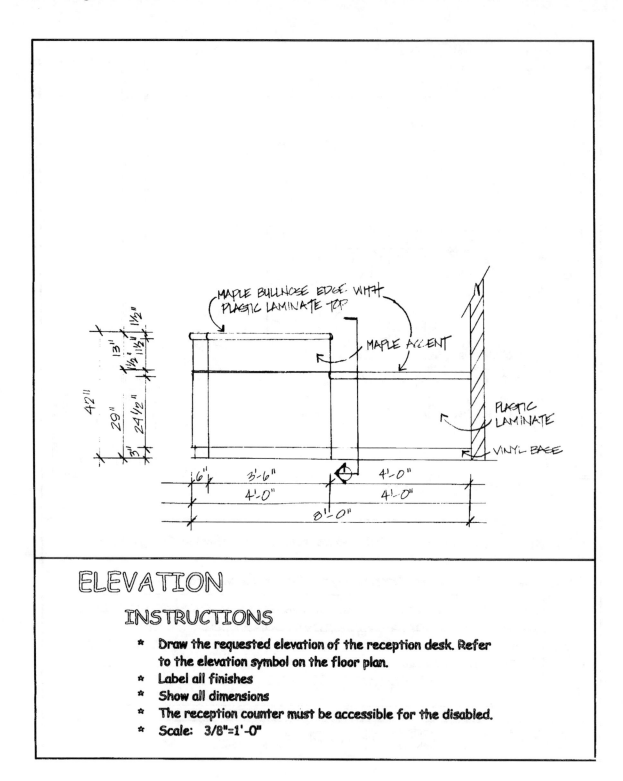

ELEVATION

INSTRUCTIONS

* Draw the requested elevation of the reception desk. Refer to the elevation symbol on the floor plan.
* Label all finishes
* Show all dimensions
* The reception counter must be accessible for the disabled.
* Scale: 3/8"=1'-0"

Figure 5.11 Elevation

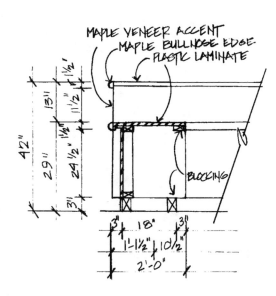

MAPLE VENEER ACCENT
MAPLE BULLNOSE EDGE
PLASTIC LAMINATE

BLOCKING

SECTION

INSTRUCTIONS

* Draw a section through the side of the desk in an area that is accessible to the disabled.
* Indicate the section with the proper symbol on the elevation drawing.
* Show dimensions.
* Indicate and label all materials to illustrate design intent.
* Scale: 3/8"=1'-0"

Figure 5.12 Section

Reading List

NCIDQ PRACTICUM REFERENCES

Ballast, David K. *Interior Design Reference Manual*. Belmont, CA: Professional Publications, Inc., 2002.

BOMA International. *ADA Compliance Guidebook*. Washington DC: BOMA International, 1992.

Ching, Francis D. K. *Building Construction Illustrated,* 3rd ed. New York: Van Nostrand Reinhold, Co., 2000.

Ching, Frank. *Architectural Graphics,* 3rd ed. New York: John Wiley & Sons, 1996.

Council of American Building Officials. CAB/ANSI A117.1-1998, *American National Standard—Accessible and Usable Buildings and Facilities*. Falls Church, VA: International Code Council, 1998.

DeChiara, J., J. Panero, and M. Zelnik. *Time Saver Standards for Interior Design and Space Planning*. New York: McGraw-Hill, Inc., 1991. **OUT OF PRINT**

Drpic, Ivo D. *Sketching and Rendering Interior Spaces—Practical Techniques for Professional Results*. New York: Whitney Library of Design, 1988.

Falcone, Joseph D. *Architectural Drawing & Design: Principles and Practices*. Englewood Cliffs, NJ: Prentice Hall, 1990. **OUT OF PRINT**

Gordon, Gary, and James Nuckolls. *Interior Lighting for Designers*. New York: John Wiley & Sons, 1995.

National Council for Interior Design Qualification. *NCIDQ Examination Guide*. Washington, DC, 2000.

Pile, John F. *Interior Design*. New York: Harry N. Abrahams, Inc., 1988.

Ramsey, Charles George and Harold Reeve Sleeper. *Architectural Graphic Standards,* 10th ed. ed. Robert T. Packard, AIA. New York: Wiley Publications, 2000.

Reznikoff, S. C. *Interior Graphic and Design Standards*. New York: Whitney Library of Design/Watson-Guptill Publications, 1986.

_____. *Specifications for Commercial Interiors.* New York: Whitney Library of Design/Watson-Guptill Publications, 1989.

Rupp, William and Arnold Friedmann. *Construction Materials for Interior Design: Principles of Structure and Properties of Materials.* New York: Watson-Guptill Publications, 1989.

Smith, Fran Kellogg, and Fred J. Bertolone. *Bringing Interiors to Light.* New York: Watson-Guptill Publications, 1986.

BIBLIOGRAPHY

Briggs, L., and W. Wager. *Handbook of Procedures for the Design of Instruction,* 2nd ed. Englewood Cliffs, NJ: Educational Technology Publications, 1981.

Council of American Building Officials. ICC/ANSI A117.1-1998, *American National Standard—Accessible and Usable Buildings and Facilities.* Falls Church, VA: International Code Council, 1998.

Dick, W., and L. Carey. *The Systematic Design of Instruction,* 5th ed. Addison-Wesley Publishing, 2000.

Dubois, P., and G. Mayo. *The Complete Book of Training: Theory, Principles, and Techniques.* San Diego: University Publications, 1987.

Finrow, G., ed. *ASID Step: Self-Testing Exercises for Pre-Professionals Workbook.* Washington DC: G. Finrow, 1993.

National Council for Interior Design Qualification. *NCIDQ Examination Guide.* Washington, DC, 2000.

National Council for Interior Design Qualification. *Report of the Job Analysis of Interior Design.* New York: NCIDQ, 1991.

Phillips, J. *Handbook of Training Evaluation and Measurement Methods.* Houston: Gulf Publishing, 1987. **OUT OF PRINT**

Ramsey, Charles George, Harold Reeve Sleeper, and John Ray Hoke, Jr. *Architectural Graphic Standards,* 10th ed. New York: John Wiley & Sons, 2000.

Shumaker, Terrence and David Madsen. *Autocad and Its Applications.* Goodheart-Wilcox Co., Inc., 2001.

Sommer, B., and R. Sommer. *A Practical Guide to Behavioral Research: Tools and Techniques,* 5th ed. New York: Oxford University Press, 2001.

www.ncidq.org